Sailing Club, 3rd edition
© 2024, Anna Frazier

All rights reserved. This book or any portion thereof may not be reproduced or used in any manner whatsoever without the author's express written permission, except for the use of quotations in a book review.

Poems
Published 2024
Edited with Sophie Medvick

Sailing Club

also by anna frazier

Elizabeth Young: The Mind's Mess (2020)
The Moon Reaches For Me (2020)
Thank You For The Flowers (2021)
Violet Afternoon (2021)
Adaptations (2022)
Snow Hills (2023)
Befriending Longing (2023)

view the most updated list of collections
at annafrazierpoetry.com.

POEMS

by anna frazier

connect

visit annafrazierpoetry.com to subscribe to email updates on her new collections, view featured poems, and learn more about the author.

note from the author

these books are meant to be read in order and from left to right. welcome to a new space.

dedication

for survivors of chronic pain

introduction

this book is about the journey none of us agreed to take with chronic conditions. so many people are members of a club where we sail vessels of illness forever, be it mental, physical, or other kinds. this book is a place where you are not alone in that suffering, because i feel the everydayness of it too.

maybe you are not a member of this club but know someone in it. perhaps this book can give you insight into what that person may deal with — maybe in silence.

lastly, this book is meant to call attention to the pain we all quietly endure each day, unbeknownst to those around us. in a coffee shop, in traffic, working from home, waiting tables… pain is everywhere. let us live kindly and consider that those nearby may be hurting — hurting so much and so often that it feels like the people in our circles no longer feel the weight of this burden we carry each living moment.

contents

dry as a dream 1
the club 2
the animal 3
pain is a wind 4
what keeps me alive 5
becoming the pain 6
overdose 7
joy is a sin 8
the paradox of understanding 9
symptoms of living 10
i'm superhuman without my pain 11
"on my way" 12
the rabbit 13
spoon theory 14
the other halves 15
mine 16
prescriptions 17
piling 18
barbie 19
chronic pain 20
he loves me, he loves me not 21
what if suffering was a sticker 22
giving up 23

"americans with disabilities" 24
what revives me 25
the antidote 26
the paradox of paralysis 27
too much 28

acknowledgments 31
reviews 33

dry as a dream

dreaming is what keeps me going.
longing pulls me through the waves
of day-in-day-out pain, indescribable
to the ordinary person. pain has no limit;
neither does the imagination. if the pain
can be great, so can the dreams. pain dries up
the determination to move, the ambition to achieve
great things. victory becomes any moment
enveloped in a dream. while i lay, a tattered sail,
draped on the sofa, dry as a dream, the bubbling foam
of imagined, painless worlds survives me.

the chronic painers — we have a club
of invisible survivors. while other people
sail through life on effortless limbs
in painless modes, members
of the sailing club pay everyday
just to belong. it's expensive
to be in our club. the daily toll
of perseverance coupled with
the mask of okayness
is exhausting. being alone
has this solace where our pain
needn't be explained
to every curious, caring person.
so lonely, though, to belong to our club.
who around can understand
we're not in a "mood,"
we're "okay," but we're not,
and, yes, if they had to live this way,
they could, even as they marvel
at our strength and courage.

the club

the animal

the animal is our favorite.
the animal cannot speak, ask
how we're feeling, admire us
for our superhuman strength
to continue, or frown
at our eternal discomfort —
the animal can only observe.

pain is a wind

it blows in a continuous movement
across me, over me, through me.
the wind doesn't see me.
it blows when it wishes
at its most selfish severity.
it knows no life except persistence,
nothing of love or dreams.

what keeps me alive

the dream that someday i will live.
someday, i will truly live,
like people do who don't carry pain
every waking moment. the dream
that i will live one day out of all the days
without pain. the dream of a painless
twelve hours, even a painless six.
prayer, roses, ice, the animal.

becoming the pain

clouds have replaced my spine.
when i lean back into the sky,
i dissolve into the endlessness
of myself — a ghost in the snow
reduced to one shade: pain.

overdose

after a full day of work, i prepare to study. hours later,
my eyelashes sweep the floor as i wake to a bottle
in my hand. the bottle has tilted, spilling pills
in a little mountain. my memory-fog tumbles
backward in time, and i remember the pain
lulling me to sleep while i tried to contain it
in the little bottle. now, the evening has folded
into a black midnight. there is no time to study,
no mental reserve either.

joy is a sin

i think i'll go out and smell the poppies.
   the patio edge — as far as my pain will allow.
i bend down to see the colors,
   but i cannot get back up.

the paradox of understanding

chronic pain is the only color
my pen has yet to paint.
writing is an escape from my pain,
unless the writing is about the pain.
something is easy
in my story being heard;
something is hard
in telling it.

symptoms of living

today, the migraine is quiet.
it sews ropes out of my jaw muscles,
sits patiently on my cheekbones,
presses a finger to each one of my teeth.
the migraine is like a freckle on my skin —
it is a part of me, and the thought
of its absence is silly.

i'm superhuman without my pain

i go in for a job interview.
they watch me work:
my talent wears a large coat
made of aching wool.
my whole body moves
through invisible water, my eyes
shaded by the migraine.
i reach for drinking glasses
that aren't there and forget
where i'm taking the ice cream
by the time i get up the stairs.

"*on my way*" the nausea
unties my shoelaces
while the pain presses its hands
over my eyes. tension binds my jaw
shut as if clenched,
but it's not.

the rabbit

does a rabbit sit atop my head?
it never lets me out of bed.
it tosses its crown,
not getting up or down,
twiddling its tail all around.

to non-members of the sailing club:

spoons are energy, let's say.
we all get the same amount
of spoons each day.

spoon theory

i wake up, still in bed, with the rabbit
on my head. that pain takes a spoon
    from me, so i have one less unit free.
     i get up, eat an egg, dragging my rabbit
      by the leg. you enjoy the food you make
       while i distract from this ravenous ache.
       the joy taken from my meal steals a spoon
      for that ordeal. i can't pick up anything
     new with those two occupied spoons.
what might've taken you just one
every morning takes me two.
now i have fewer than you.
my spoons hold the toll
of the energy pain takes
— i'm full.

the other halves

let's not forget the other halves
that hear us cry day after day,
say how much we wish
to die. the other halves
have their own lasting pain,
watching us wither
and waste away.

i have a few halves. don't do the math.
some of my halves roam the earth,
there for me with internet words.
  but one of my halves is here
mine on the couch in a constant state
    of giving out hugs and cooked soups,
even help with washing the spoons.
thank you to the half that's here
for catching every one of my tears.

prescriptions

even as i write this book,
the pills give me deceiving looks.
they say they'll swallow up my hurt,
but they don't match
their stated worth.
i take them anyway in case
they work and lift my ache.
snap an x-ray — it'll show
i'm the bottle filled with woe.

imagine —
jenga blocks stacked mile-high
reach a level unmet by
round rock-stacks at the river.

my emotional foundation quivers
from the bottom, bent down
at the edges by the frown
forced upon me from the pain.

piling

other people stack their days
or stressful blocks like bricks
in layers. but we sailors on our ships
cannot stack with stable rise
the undulating life events that try
our inner strength and yours.

we both start with the same first block,
but mine's wobbly, and yours is not.
stack a difficult day at work,
heartbreak, or grief, some kind of hurt —
mine will fall where yours may not.

the way they pile differs alot.

barbie

i'm going to get wrinkles before you
from every line my nails have carved
into my face to move the pain.
my hair will fall out too soon
from all the times i've bunched it up
in my fists and pulled it as hard as i can.

chronic pain

chronic pain is anything, right?
chronic pain can be grief for many years
if that's what it is for you.
chronic pain is simply the rabbit —
a weight that sits on you,
stubborn and without shifting.
it can take many forms.

he loves me, he loves me not

i am not just a medicine cocktail.
i am just a medicine cocktail.
i am not a burden to my friends and family.
i am a burden to my friends and family.
i am more dynamic than my pain.
i am not more dynamic than my pain.

what if suffering was a sticker

what if we all wore
our pain labels
on our foreheads?
i wonder how
our conversations
would change.

chronic pain means
constantly crossing things off my list
that i used to be able to do

no more long runs up the mountain
    no more skiing or high altitude
    no more out to eat

giving up

it's like i've aged fifty years
but i'm still in this body

giving up more of it
giving up more on it

"americans with disabilities"

it's illegal to fire someone
for their disability.
so instead, my employers
have chosen to give me "special treatment."
less hours, so i don't get "overwhelmed."
they tell me to go home,
to "take care" of myself.
this isn't so much a poem
as it is a reality.

"why did you choose me?"
i ask my favorite person.
"because you're the only one
that understands me."

what revives me

understanding you has pulled me
like a rope out of my first and deepest
depression all the way through
the ten years of life that have followed.

understanding you is tied around my wrist.
it's like an emergency cord you can pull
when i fall into a hole — when my pain
covers my eyes, when i don't even know
the point of living if i'm not living at all.

remind me that i understand you,
and i will stand up.

the antidote

"the insurance won't cover it,
but you can't get it
for less than two thousand dollars
by cash. if you skip rent
this month, perhaps you can be free
from your pain for a third of a day."

the paradox of paralysis

what if the only thing you want to do is the thing that causes the pain, and the only thing to ease the pain is the horizontal state you find yourself in from such an action.

chronic pain makes people see you
differently. they just see the pain,
they don't see the person. they see
all the sacrifices they'll have to make
to be with you instead of all the joy
you bring to the world. they say
too much it's too much, or you're too much,
or offer some version of your-pain
-making-you-not-good-enough.

is being written-off the cost
of membership into the sailing club?

now i am the other half.
suddenly after a laugh,
i watch him cry the rest of the day,
say how he wishes to die.

it's bad for me, but it's worse for you

between hoping he survives,
i wash myself in the absence
of his true essence,
praying for its return,
knowing that pain
has erased his presence,
leaving a pile of bones
for this world. *i love you
any form you take,
a pile of bones
or a vibrant wave.*
i'm sorry you're a member here,
and i wish i could pay your dues.
i will always wash your tears
and return them folded, warm,
and new.

acknowledgments

thank you to all who have supported me
in my journey with chronic migraine.

thank you to my parents for paying the expenses
of endless new doctors and medications.

thank you to nurtec, emgality, and cefaly
for getting me closer to healing than ever before.

thank you to my editor for being a member of this club
with me and understanding the price.

review

leave a review of this collection on
annafrazierpoetry.com in the "contact" section.

reviews help the author's collection to be viewable by a wider audience, so others can share the experience that you have just had reading the collection.

www.ingramcontent.com/pod-product-compliance
Lightning Source LLC
LaVergne TN
LVHW031614060526
838201LV00065B/4841